Decarbonizing Shipping: Pathways to Zero Emissions

Contents

Preface
Introduction

Prelude
Chapter 1: The Need for Decarbonization
Chapter 2:Pathways to Decarbonization
Chapter 3: Role of Technology and Innovation
Chapter 4: Regulatory and Policy Landscape
Chapter 5: Financing the Transition
Chapter 6: Challenges and Barriers to Decarbonization
Chapter 7: Future Outlook and Case Studies
Conclusion:The Road to Zero Emissions
Glossary

Preface

The maritime industry is undergoing a significant transformation as the global push for decarbonization accelerates. With stricter regulations, emerging technologies, and the increasing pressure to meet sustainability goals, shipping companies are facing the challenge of drastically reducing carbon emissions. Recognizing the need for a practical and accessible resource, *Decarbonizing Shipping: Pathways to Zero Emissions* provides a comprehensive look at the tools, technologies, and strategies that will shape the future of a zero-emission maritime sector.

This book, part of the Gosships Learning Series, is designed for industry professionals seeking to navigate the complexities of decarbonization. It offers foundational to intermediate knowledge, with an emphasis on real-world applications and emerging regulatory frameworks. Every chapter is crafted to empower maritime and offshore personnel with the insights necessary to make informed decisions that align with both environmental standards and operational efficiency.

Our goal is to equip maritime professionals, from entry-level crew to seasoned shoreside managers, with the tools they need to succeed in the evolving landscape of sustainable shipping. We hope this resource contributes to your professional development and supports your commitment to leading the industry toward a greener future.

Introduction

Welcome to *Decarbonizing Shipping: Pathways to Zero Emissions*, a book designed to help maritime professionals understand the pathways to a more sustainable future. As part of the Gosships Learning Series, this book provides up-to-date insights from industry experts and regulators, ensuring the content is both reliable and applicable to the challenges you face.

In this book, we explore:

- **The Importance of Decarbonization**: Understand the driving forces behind the push to reduce emissions in shipping.
- **Alternative Fuels**: Dive into the growing role of green fuels like ammonia, hydrogen, methanol, and biofuels.
- **Renewable Energy in Shipping**: Explore how renewable energy sources can be integrated into maritime operations.
- **Carbon Capture and Storage**: Learn about the potential for carbon capture technologies to mitigate shipping emissions.
- **Regulatory Compliance**: Understand the evolving regulatory frameworks that are pushing the industry toward zero emissions.
- **Case Studies**: Real-world examples of companies leading the way in decarbonizing their fleets.

After reading this book, you'll have the opportunity to test your knowledge through a certification exam, validating your expertise in decarbonization strategies. Successful completion will earn you a Certificate of Achievement, available through the Gosships training platform at www.gosships.com.

Who is this book for?

This book is for:

- Maritime professionals seeking to deepen their understanding of decarbonization strategies.
- Shoreside managers aiming to implement sustainable practices in

shipping operations.

- Students and aspiring professionals eager to build a career in the evolving maritime and energy sectors.

- Government officials and regulators looking to stay informed about decarbonization trends and policies in the maritime industry.

By mastering the concepts outlined in this book, you'll be equipped to lead the transition to cleaner shipping practices, ensuring compliance with international regulations and contributing to a more sustainable future for the maritime industry.

Thank you for choosing the Gosships Learning Series as a resource on your journey toward professional growth and sustainable operations.

Gosships Learning Series 2024/2025

1. Hydrogen: The Fuel of the Future
2. Green Ammonia: The Next Big Thing in Shipping
3. Decarbonizing Shipping: Pathways to Zero Emissions
4. Battery Technology for Industrial Applications
5. Carbon Capture and Storage: Can It Save the Planet?
6. Biofuels 101: Turning Waste into Energy
7. Understanding LNG (Liquefied Natural Gas)
8. Methanol as a Marine Fuel
9. Offshore Wind Energy: The Future of Renewable Power
10. Tidal and Wave Energy: Harnessing the Ocean
11. Electrofuels: The Next Generation of Carbon-Neutral Fuels
12. Energy Storage Systems for Grid Reliability
13. Hydrogen Fuel Cells for Transportation
14. Solar Energy Innovations: Beyond Solar Panels
15. Smart Grids: The Backbone of Future Energy Systems
16. Ammonia-Hydrogen Blends: A Dual Fuel Solution?
17. Nuclear Power: Small Modular Reactors for a Low-Carbon Future
18. Hydropower: The Oldest Renewable Energy Source
19. Decentralized Energy Systems: Microgrids for Resilience
20. Energy Efficiency Technologies for Industry
21. Hydrogen Production from Seawater
22. Fuel Cells for Maritime Applications
23. Geothermal Energy: Unlocking Earth's Heat
24. Future of EV Charging Infrastructure
25. Synthetic Fuels: Bridging the Gap to Decarbonization
26. Cybersecurity for Maritime and Offshore Operations

27. AI and Automation in Shipping and Logistics
28. Digital Twins in Maritime: Revolutionizing Asset Management
29. Risk Management in Offshore and Maritime Operations
30. Compliance with IMO 2020 Regulations
31. Sustainable Ship Design: Reducing Environmental Impact
32. Marine Renewable Energy: Wave, Tidal, and Offshore Wind Integration
33. Ballast Water Management Systems
34. Blockchain Technology in Shipping: Improving Transparency & Efficiency
35. Effective Supply Chain Management for Energy Industries
36. Leadership in the Energy Transition
37. Effective Crisis Management in Maritime Operations
38. Shipyard Safety Management Systems
39. Port State Control (PSC) Inspection Readiness
40. Remote Vessel Operations and Autonomous Shipping
41. Optimizing Fleet Performance with Data Analytics
42. Maritime Environmental Regulations: Staying Ahead of Compliance
43. Advanced Maintenance Strategies: Condition Monitoring & Predictive Maintenance
44. Global LNG Market: Trends and Opportunities
45. Incident Investigation in Maritime Operations
46. International Maritime Law: Key Concepts and Applications
47. Emergency Preparedness and Response for Offshore Oil & Gas
48. Energy Transition Strategies for Oil and Gas Companies
49. Maritime Drones: Applications and Safety Considerations
50. Effective Project Management in Offshore Energy Projects

All Rights Reserved Disclaimer

The contents of this book, including but not limited to all text, graphics, images, logos, and designs, are the intellectual property of Gosships LLC and are protected by copyright law. No part of this publication may be reproduced, distributed, transmitted, displayed, or modified in any form or by any means, including photocopying, recording, or other electronic or mechanical methods, without the prior written permission of the publisher, except in the case of brief quotations in critical reviews or articles.

The information contained within this book is for educational purposes only and is provided "as is" without warranty of any kind, either expressed or implied. The authors and publishers disclaim any liability for any direct, indirect, or consequential loss or damage arising from the use of the material in this book.

For permissions or inquiries, please contact: admin@gosships.com

© 2024 Gosships LLC. All rights reserved.

Prelude

Shipping is one of the most critical components of global trade, carrying nearly 90% of goods worldwide. As economies grow and international trade increases, the demand for shipping services rises. However, with this growing importance comes a significant environmental responsibility. The shipping industry is one of the largest sources of greenhouse gas (GHG) emissions, contributing to global warming and climate change.

The International Maritime Organization (IMO) has set ambitious targets for reducing these emissions. Specifically, the IMO aims to reduce total GHG emissions from international shipping by at least 50% by 2050 compared to 2008 levels, with the ultimate goal of achieving net-zero emissions. This book outlines the various pathways to decarbonize shipping, including advancements in technology, alternative fuels, and regulatory frameworks, providing a practical roadmap for professionals and enthusiasts seeking to understand the future of the industry.

Decarbonizing shipping is not just about meeting regulatory requirements; it is about securing the future of the industry in a world increasingly focused on sustainability. By reducing emissions, shipping companies can not only comply with international regulations but also gain a competitive advantage in a market where environmental responsibility is becoming a key factor in business decisions.

Chapter 1

The Need for Decarbonization

Shipping's impact on the environment cannot be ignored. Carbon dioxide (CO_2), nitrogen oxides (NO_x), sulfur oxides (SO_x), and particulate matter from ships contribute significantly to air pollution and global warming. CO_2 emissions, in particular, are a major concern due to their role in the greenhouse effect, which leads to global temperature increases and extreme weather patterns.

The IMO and other international organizations are driving the push for decarbonization in the shipping sector. The Paris Agreement, signed in 2015, aims to limit global temperature increases to well below 2°C above pre-industrial levels, with efforts to limit the increase to 1.5°C. To meet these targets, it is essential that all sectors, including shipping, drastically reduce their emissions.

Moreover, the health impacts of shipping emissions are increasingly being recognized. Communities near major shipping routes or ports are exposed to higher levels of air pollution, leading to respiratory problems and other health issues. Reducing emissions is not only about combating climate change but also about improving public health.

In addition to regulatory pressure, there is growing market demand for greener shipping solutions. Consumers and businesses are becoming more environmentally conscious, and companies with sustainable practices are often seen as more attractive partners. For shipping companies, decarbonization offers the opportunity to enhance their reputation and attract eco-conscious customers.

Chapter 2

Pathways to Decarbonization

Decarbonizing the shipping industry requires a multi-faceted approach. No single solution will achieve the necessary reductions in emissions, but several pathways can work together to bring the industry closer to zero emissions.

Energy Efficiency

Improving the energy efficiency of ships is one of the most effective ways to reduce emissions. Existing vessels can be retrofitted with more efficient engines, advanced propellers, and optimized hull designs to reduce drag and improve fuel efficiency. Slow steaming, where ships operate at reduced speeds, is another technique that can significantly cut fuel consumption. However, this practice must be balanced with operational and economic considerations, as slower voyages can increase delivery times.

In addition, improving the operational efficiency of shipping fleets through better scheduling, route optimization, and maintenance practices can lead to further reductions in fuel use and emissions. For example, advanced weather routing systems can help ships avoid rough seas, reducing energy consumption.

Fuel Substitutes

The transition to alternative fuels is a key component of shipping's decarbonization strategy. While liquefied natural gas (LNG) is currently a popular option due to its lower CO_2 emissions compared to conventional marine fuels, it is still a fossil fuel and only offers a partial solution. The focus is now shifting toward zero-carbon fuels such as green ammonia, hydrogen, and biofuels.

- **Green Ammonia**: Ammonia can be produced using renewable energy, offering a potential zero-emission fuel for ships. However, challenges include ammonia's toxicity, storage, and energy density.
- **Hydrogen**: Hydrogen is another promising zero-carbon fuel. When produced using renewable energy, it can be stored as a gas or in liquid form and used in fuel cells to generate electricity. However, hydrogen requires significant infrastructure development for storage, transport, and bunkering.
- **Methanol**: Methanol, particularly when derived from renewable sources, is another option being explored. It has the advantage of being easier to store and handle than hydrogen or ammonia, but it is less energy-dense.

Each of these alternative fuels presents both opportunities and challenges, and their widespread adoption will depend on technological advances, cost reductions, and the development of global bunkering infrastructure.

Electrification and Hybrid Systems

Electrification, particularly for short-sea shipping and ferries, is becoming increasingly viable. Battery-powered vessels are already in operation, providing zero-emission transport for shorter routes. Hybrid systems, which combine batteries with traditional engines or fuel cells, offer a flexible solution, allowing ships to operate on cleaner power in areas where emissions are restricted, such as ports, while using conventional fuels for longer ocean voyages.

Shore power, also known as cold ironing, allows ships to turn off their engines while docked and use electricity from the grid instead. This reduces emissions in port areas, where air quality concerns are often most pressing. Several ports worldwide are already investing in the infrastructure needed to provide shore power to visiting vessels.

Carbon Capture and Storage (CCS)

Carbon capture and storage (CCS) is another emerging technology with the potential to significantly reduce shipping emissions. CCS systems capture CO_2 from ship exhaust and store it either on board or transfer it to storage facilities on land. While still in the experimental stage, CCS could become a key tool in reducing emissions from ships that continue to use fossil fuels during the transition to cleaner alternatives.

Chapter 3

Role of Technology and Innovation

Innovation will play a crucial role in achieving shipping's decarbonization goals. Several emerging technologies are already being deployed, with the potential to transform the industry.

Digitalization and Smart Shipping

Digital technologies such as artificial intelligence (AI), big data analytics, and the Internet of Things (IoT) can optimize vessel operations, improving fuel efficiency and reducing emissions. For example, AI-powered route optimization tools can analyze real-time weather and sea conditions, adjusting routes to minimize fuel consumption. Similarly, predictive maintenance systems can monitor the condition of critical ship components, preventing inefficiencies caused by equipment failure.

Smart shipping solutions also include real-time monitoring systems that provide operators with detailed data on fuel consumption, engine performance, and emissions. This allows for more precise management of ship operations, helping to reduce fuel use and emissions.

Automation

Autonomous ships, which operate with minimal or no human intervention, are another promising development. By using advanced sensors, AI, and navigation systems, these vessels can operate more efficiently than conventional ships, reducing fuel consumption and emissions. While fully autonomous ships are still in development, semi-autonomous vessels are already being tested, and their adoption could accelerate as the technology matures.

Advanced Hull Coatings and Materials

Innovations in ship design and materials can also contribute to decarbonization. Advanced hull coatings that reduce friction between the ship's hull and the water can lead to significant fuel savings. These coatings are designed to prevent biofouling, which occurs when marine organisms such as algae and barnacles attach to the hull, increasing drag and fuel consumption.

New materials such as lightweight composites are being used in shipbuilding to reduce vessel weight, which also improves fuel efficiency.

These materials offer the added benefit of increased durability, reducing the need for frequent maintenance and repairs.

Chapter 4
Regulatory and Policy Landscape

The regulatory framework surrounding shipping emissions is rapidly evolving. The IMO's GHG strategy is the primary driver of international efforts to reduce emissions in the shipping industry. The IMO has introduced several measures aimed at improving ship efficiency and reducing emissions, including:

- **Energy Efficiency Design Index (EEDI)**: This regulation applies to new ships and sets mandatory efficiency standards that vary depending on the type of ship.

- **Ship Energy Efficiency Management Plan (SEEMP)**: This requires all ships to implement a management plan to improve energy efficiency and reduce emissions.

- **Carbon Intensity Indicator (CII)**: The CII framework measures a ship's efficiency in terms of CO_2 emissions per cargo tonne-mile. Ships must meet progressively stricter CII requirements.

Regional regulations are also shaping the decarbonization landscape. For example, the European Union's Emissions Trading System (ETS) will soon include maritime emissions, requiring shipowners to purchase allowances for their CO_2 emissions. This creates a financial incentive for companies to reduce emissions by investing in cleaner technologies and fuels.

In addition to regulatory measures, market-based mechanisms such as carbon pricing and fuel levies are being discussed. These mechanisms would make carbon-intensive fuels more expensive, encouraging the industry to transition to cleaner alternatives.

Chapter 5

Financing the Transition

Decarbonizing the shipping industry requires substantial investment. However, several financing options are available to support this transition.

Green Financing

Green bonds and sustainability-linked loans are becoming increasingly popular in the shipping sector. These financial instruments provide capital at favorable terms for companies committed to reducing their carbon emissions. For example, shipping companies can use green bonds to finance the construction of energy-efficient vessels or retrofit existing ships with cleaner technologies.

Sustainability-linked loans, which offer interest rate reductions for companies that meet specific environmental targets, are another tool that can incentivize decarbonization. By tying financial performance to sustainability metrics, these loans encourage shipowners to prioritize emission reduction efforts.

Private Capital and Institutional Investors

Institutional investors, such as pension funds and sovereign wealth funds, are increasingly prioritizing investments in sustainable industries. Shipping companies that demonstrate a commitment to decarbonization are more likely to attract investment from these sources. Several large financial institutions have also signed onto the Poseidon Principles, an initiative that aligns ship financing with the IMO's climate goals.

Chapter 6

Challenges and Barriers to Decarbonization

While the pathways to decarbonization are clear, significant challenges remain.

Technological Limitations

Many of the technologies needed to decarbonize the shipping industry, such as hydrogen-powered engines and carbon capture systems, are still in development. Widespread adoption of these technologies will require significant investment in research and development, as well as the creation of new infrastructure.

Infrastructure Gaps

The global shipping industry lacks the infrastructure needed to support the transition to cleaner fuels. For example, bunkering facilities for alternative fuels such as hydrogen or ammonia are currently limited. Ports will also need to invest in electrification infrastructure to support shore power and battery-powered ships.

Costs

Decarbonizing ships is expensive, and many shipowners are hesitant to make large capital investments in new technologies without clearer regulatory guidelines or financial incentives. The high cost of alternative fuels, compared to conventional marine fuels, is another significant barrier.

Chapter 7

Future Outlook and Case Studies

Despite the challenges, several companies are already making significant progress toward decarbonization. Case studies of industry leaders such as Maersk and CMA CGM provide valuable insights into the future of sustainable shipping.

Maersk

Maersk, one of the world's largest shipping company, has committed to achieving net-zero emissions by 2040. The company is investing in methanol-powered ships and is working to develop the infrastructure needed to support alternative fuels. Maersk's approach demonstrates the importance of long-term planning and investment in cleaner technologies.

CMA CGM

CMA CGM is another major player that is adopting LNG-powered ships as part of its decarbonization strategy. The company is also investing in carbon offset programs to further reduce its carbon footprint. CMA CGM's efforts highlight the importance of diversifying decarbonization strategies and using a combination of solutions to reduce emissions.

These case studies illustrate that while the path to decarbonization is challenging, it is achievable with the right investments, technologies, and regulatory support.

Conclusion: The Road to Zero Emissions

Decarbonizing the shipping industry is a complex and expensive task, but it is essential for the future of the planet. The pathways outlined in this book demonstrate that there are multiple approaches to reducing emissions, from improving energy efficiency to adopting alternative fuels and leveraging technological innovations.

The journey toward zero emissions will require collaboration across the entire maritime value chain, from shipowners and operators to regulators and technology providers. The transition will take time, but with sustained effort and investment, the shipping industry can play a critical role in creating a more sustainable future for global trade.

Glossary - Decarbonizing Shipping: Pathways to Zero Emissions:

1. Alternative Fuels: Fuels that are not derived from traditional petroleum sources, such as hydrogen, ammonia, biofuels, and methanol, offering lower carbon emissions.

2. Ammonia (NH_3): A carbon-free alternative fuel for shipping, produced from renewable energy sources for use in the maritime industry.

3. Ammonia Combustion: The process of burning ammonia as a fuel, producing nitrogen and water without CO_2 emissions.

4. BECCS (Bioenergy with Carbon Capture and Storage): Technology that combines bioenergy production with carbon capture to achieve negative emissions, considered a potential solution for shipping's carbon reduction.

5. Biofuels: Fuels derived from organic matter, such as plant materials or animal waste, that can be used as a renewable alternative to traditional fossil fuels in shipping.

6. Bunkering: The process of supplying ships with fuel, which will require modifications to support alternative fuels like ammonia and hydrogen.

7. Carbon Capture and Storage (CCS): A technology to capture and store CO_2 emissions from industrial processes, preventing their release into the atmosphere.

8. Carbon Intensity: A measure of the amount of CO_2 emissions produced per unit of energy or work, used as a key metric in assessing fuel efficiency.

9. Carbon Neutral: Achieving net-zero carbon emissions by balancing emitted carbon with carbon offsets or capture.

10. Carbon Tax: A tax imposed on carbon emissions to incentivize industries, including shipping, to adopt cleaner fuels and technologies.

11. CO_2 (Carbon Dioxide): A greenhouse gas primarily produced by burning fossil fuels, and a major contributor to global warming.

12. Cold Ironing: The process of providing ships with electrical power from shore while docked, reducing emissions from ship engines in port.

13. Decarbonization: The process of reducing or eliminating carbon dioxide (CO_2) emissions, particularly in industries such as shipping.

14. Direct Air Capture (DAC): A technology that captures CO_2 directly from the atmosphere, which could be used alongside carbon-neutral fuels in shipping.

15. ECA (Emission Control Area): Designated areas where stricter emissions standards are enforced to reduce air pollution from ships.

16.

17. EEDI (Energy Efficiency Design Index): A regulatory measure of a ship's energy efficiency, established by the IMO, which promotes lower emissions.

18. Electrolysis: The process of using electricity to split water into hydrogen and oxygen, a method used to produce green hydrogen for shipping fuels.

19. Emission Trading System (ETS): A market-based system where companies buy or sell allowances for emissions, potentially affecting the shipping industry.

20. GHG (Greenhouse Gases): Gases that trap heat in the atmosphere, including CO_2, methane, and nitrous oxide, contributing to climate change.

21. Green Ammonia: Ammonia produced using renewable energy sources without emitting CO_2, considered a potential zero-emission fuel for shipping.

22. Green Hydrogen: Hydrogen produced using renewable energy through electrolysis, offering a clean energy source for fuel cells and alternative fuels.

23. Greenhouse Effect: The warming of the Earth's atmosphere due to the buildup of greenhouse gases, including CO_2, from burning fossil fuels.

24. HFO (Heavy Fuel Oil): A highly polluting, viscous fuel traditionally used in shipping, which is being phased out in favor of cleaner alternatives.

25. Hydrogen (H_2): A zero-carbon fuel that can be used in fuel cells or as a feedstock for producing alternative fuels like ammonia.

26. IMO (International Maritime Organization): The United Nations agency responsible for regulating international shipping, including emissions reduction standards.

27. IMO 2020: A regulation limiting sulfur content in marine fuels to 0.5%, aimed at reducing air pollution from ships.

28. IMO GHG Strategy: The IMO's long-term strategy to reduce greenhouse gas emissions from international shipping by at least 50% by 2050.

29. LCA (Lifecycle Assessment): A process that evaluates the environmental impact of a product from its production to its disposal, used to assess alternative fuels like ammonia and hydrogen.

30. LNG (Liquefied Natural Gas): A cleaner-burning fossil fuel alternative to heavy fuel oil, often seen as a transition fuel for shipping's decarbonization.

31. Low-Carbon Fuels: Fuels that emit fewer greenhouse gases than conventional fuels, including biofuels, methanol, and liquefied natural gas.

32. Maritime Energy Transition: The global movement toward adopting renewable energy sources and alternative fuels to reduce shipping's environmental impact.

33. Methanol (CH3OH): A low-carbon alternative fuel being explored for use in shipping, produced from renewable or fossil-based sources.

34. Net Zero: Achieving a balance between emissions produced and emissions removed from the atmosphere, a target for the shipping industry by 2050.

35. NOx (Nitrogen Oxides): Harmful pollutants produced during combustion, contributing to air pollution. Alternative fuels like ammonia can reduce NOx emissions.

36. Renewable Energy: Energy derived from natural sources such as wind, solar, or hydropower, which can be used to produce clean fuels for shipping.

37. Scrubber: A technology installed on ships to reduce sulfur emissions by cleaning exhaust gases before they are released into the atmosphere.

38. SEEMP (Ship Energy Efficiency Management Plan): A plan required by the IMO to help ships improve energy efficiency and reduce emissions.

39. Selective Catalytic Reduction (SCR): A technology used to reduce NOx emissions from ship engines, often used in conjunction with alternative fuels.

40. Smart Grid: An energy system that uses digital technology to optimize the distribution and use of electricity, potentially enhancing the integration of renewable energy into port operations.

41. SOx (Sulfur Oxides): Pollutants produced from burning high-sulfur marine fuels, regulated by IMO 2020 to protect air quality and reduce acid rain.

42. Sustainable Fuels: Fuels derived from renewable or waste sources that offer lower environmental impact and reduced carbon emissions compared to traditional fuels.

43. Synthetic Fuels: Fuels created from renewable electricity and captured carbon dioxide or hydrogen, offering a potential zero-emission solution for shipping.

44. Tidal Energy: A form of renewable energy derived from ocean tides, which could play a role in powering ports or providing auxiliary power to ships.

45. Well-to-Wake: A lifecycle assessment approach that considers all emissions from fuel production to its final use in the propulsion of a ship, important in evaluating alternative fuels.

46. Zero-Carbon Shipping: The goal of eliminating carbon emissions from the global shipping industry through the use of alternative fuels, renewable energy, and advanced technologies.

47. Zero-Emission Fuels (ZEF): Fuels that emit no greenhouse gases during combustion or use, such as green hydrogen and ammonia.

48. Zero-Emission Vessel (ZEV): A vessel that operates without emitting greenhouse gases, utilizing alternative fuels and technologies to achieve this goal.

49. ZEV Strategy: A long-term plan to develop, promote, and deploy zero-emission vessels in the maritime industry to meet decarbonization targets.

50. Zero-Emission Ports: Ports that aim to eliminate emissions by utilizing renewable energy sources, electrification, and smart grid technologies for their operations.

51. Zero-Emission Technologies: Technologies that enable shipping operations without the release of greenhouse gases, including battery systems, hydrogen fuel cells, and carbon-neutral fuels.

www.ingramcontent.com/pod-product-compliance
Lightning Source LLC
Chambersburg PA
CBHW030109230526
45471CB00003B/1334